Thrive During Uncertain Times

Published by Jimmie Davis Compton, Jr.

Printed in the United States of America

Publisher's Cataloging-in-Publication Data

Compton, Jimmie Davis, Jr., 1951-

Thrive During Uncertain Times / Jimmie Davis Compton, Jr.

ISBN: 978-0-940123-09-0

As uncertainty and anticipation fuel fears of losing the normalcy believers are accustomed to, desperation can easily set in. This book is concerned with the potential for such experiences to erode one's sense of self-worth and perception of who they are. It is a guide for Christians who find once reliable and stabilizing resources unavailable, and offers the assurance that they can not only survive but thrive through it all.

First Edition

Cover photo by Jimmie D. Compton, Jr.

Table of Contents

Preface

Few things reveal the true identity of a person or nation's character more than times of uncertainty. Such times expose the lows they will descend to in a quest for normalcy, or the heights they will reach for in order to uphold genuine concern for the sanctity of human life. Since the COVID-19 pandemic, uncertainty in politics (at all levels); the economy; employment; ethnic equality; constitutional order; and Christian "duty" have caused so much disorder and disruption. Normal routines in those areas will likely never return. Careers have abruptly ended, prices have skyrocketed, institutions have been dismantled and unemployment has risen. Confusion about what to do can set in and render a person vulnerable to the wiles of wishful thinking. Frustration from the inability to be relied upon by family turns into desperation; and perhaps malice. Depression can lead to despair, and a loss of hope among those who depend on caregivers or providers. Anger, paranoia and intolerance will abound. A diminished sense of worth and an identity crisis begin to taint what you think of yourself. Neither family, clergy, nor therapy seem to bring relief to the state of fugue you are walking in during these times. Then, when you need the Lord most, He seems to not even care, or to be non-existent.

This is when a healthy reminder of who you actually are, becomes essential for navigating life's rises and drops, winds, draughts, floods and burdens. Otherwise, emotions would get scrabbled like balls in a lottery scrambler. Knowing who you are, is the north star that introspectively sets boundaries for how depressed or excited you will get. Without that reminder, all that is left is positive thinking, empty clichés, motivational affirmations, religious platitudes, or other established dogma intended to keep you happy in the moment.

Your thinking becomes extreme – *Had I taken that job in the other department, things would be different* - Or, - *Had I started in this field earlier, I would have had more experience and would have kept my job.* It is too late to relocate. Besides, it may not be a matter of being in the wrong place. Time travel is not possible, so you cannot go back in time to make a different decision. Furthermore, to change the circumstances that created your crisis would involve changing the heart of an organization or of people who do not want to change. Both are unlikely.

After exhausting all options from extreme thinking, you have one more move – to reevaluate your perspective about what is happening. My favorite piece of advice to offer teenagers is; "*If you ask the wrong question, you'll get the wrong answer. If I asked you; How long is red? ... whatever measurement you reply with will be wrong.*" So during a crisis, don't ask; *Why me Lord? Why did you allow this to happen?* Instead, ask yourself, *Since Jesus urged us not to worry (Matthew 6:25-34), how can I be of service to Him while not worrying during my uncertainty?* You can, and probably should, pray about this. However, the answer is usually obvious. Any difficulty, that you might have, will probably not be genuine confusion about how to serve Him, but an unwillingness on your part to do what He asks!

As you will read later, the Lord's ways are not our ways. Your obedience is essential! Your understanding might follow later.

Lemons

Introduction: Crises in Joseph's Life

Let go from the job? Got divorced? Venturing out on your own? Unemployed? Kicked out of the house? Relocation gone bad? No matter the reason, not being in control of your destiny feels sickening and un-American. Let that feeling be the first indication that you are in need of otherworldly resources.

The evil one seeks to invade the space that was once filled with the security of a steady paycheck, benefits, comrades and a career path, with FUD (fear, uncertainty and doubt). Once in, he connects his FUD appliances to your imagination, in order to create anxiety that will degrade your health. Doing so before you can fill that space with assurances from the Lord's possibilities and promises, will make it easier for him to influence your decisions (even though he lacks the power to take that space outright). Though no one wants to descend to the lows that the evil one wants to take them to, how to prevent that is not always clear. The hope of this book is to present you with an otherworldly perspective, from a heavenly resource, so you can make lemonade from life's lemons.

Few people in the Bible faced attacks and challenges to their sense of worth and identity like Joseph. As the favorite son, Joseph was a firecracker and a tattletale. To make matters worse, after the Lord ignited a spark in the boy, it deepened the hatred from his brothers. The resulting ebbs and flows of life moved him in and out of diverse crises. But Joseph believed what the Lord had said about him through his dreams. He was not fixated on maintaining a particular facade, occupation or status. Through several crises, Joseph was forced to redefine himself occupationally in order to maintain what the Lord had sparked in him. He never lost sight of what God had revealed in the two dreams. Joseph believed that *he was, who God said he was!*

Consider the following crises of Joseph, and then imagine the uncertainty they would create.

His "Father's Favorite Son" Crises

According to scripture, the normal routines of Joseph's life were heavily colored by both, being the favorite son and hatred from his brothers. Being a tattletale (Genesis 37:2-4) certainly did not help his cause. It is safe to assume that his experiences (and do not to forget the multi-colored robe from his dad), significantly elevated Joseph's sense of worth and identity.

His "Rebuke and Disdain of Brothers" Crises

Joseph's sense of normalcy took an elevated shift. For those of you who have studied his life, there is nothing to suggest that after his dreams he became arrogant or narcissistic. The dreams were a veiled revelation from the Lord about his future. Though obscure, they were specific enough to reveal him with greater authority as compared to the rest of his family members. Without a doubt, the dream elevated his sense of worth and identity all the more. This new identity manifested itself in daily routines with his father, mother, and brothers (who really hated him), creating a new normal (Genesis 37:5-11).

His "Dark and Empty Well" Crises

Good times were about to end! Due to no fault of his own, Joseph's sense of normalcy shifted again, but not in a favorable way. His family perceived him as being condescending rather than his dream being a prophecy. And the Lord did not provide clarity, nor did He prevent Joseph from being abused by his own brothers. They grabbed Joseph and threw him into an empty well. Regardless of how painful and depressed he may have felt lying at the bottom of that well, the Lord had allowed it (Genesis 37:23-24).

His "Sold to Nomads" Crises

I imagine it is not easy to feel worthy or favored while alone, in the dark, at the bottom of a well. Today, you and I have the benefit of reading Psalm 139 to understand the omniscience of the Lord. The psalmist wrote:

> "Where can I go from your Spirit?
> Where can I flee from your presence?
> If I go up to the heavens, you are there;
> if I make my bed in the depths, you are there.
> If I rise on the wings of the dawn,
> if I settle on the far side of the sea,
> even there your hand will guide me,
> your right hand will hold me fast.
> If I say, "Surely the darkness will hide me
> and the light become night around me,"
> even the darkness will not be dark to you; the
> the night will shine like the day,
> for darkness is as light to you."
> Psalm 139:7-12

Unfortunately, during Joseph's era, that Psalm had not yet been composed. All he had were the dreams.

Fortunately, as his brothers sat to eat a meal, the Omniscient Lord sent help in the form of a caravan of Ishmaelites coming from Gilead. Though Joseph had been thrown into a well, the Lord orchestrated a way out. *Why?* As you will see later, it was because of Joseph's role in the Lord's plan for the children of Israel. As terrible as his situation of life was, his trust in what the Lord had revealed about him was key to Joseph getting through it. When his needs were in alignment with the Lord's needs, Joseph was never out of the Lord's sight. There's a message for you in that point!

Needless to say, as a purchased commodity, normalcy for Joseph had definitely shifted. Scripture does not describe how this shift affected his sense of worth and identity. Perhaps a depiction of his demeanor, as he emerges from being a commodity to becoming a servant in Egypt, will shed some light on the subject (Genesis 37:25-28).

His "Servant to Egyptian Captain" His

Still in bondage, and sold to Pharaoh's captain of the guard Potiphar, Joseph emerged as a blessing to Potiphar's household. Allowing the Lord to continue to use him, everything Joseph did in Potiphar's household succeeded. So impressed by Joseph's ability, Potiphar left everything he had in Joseph's care and under his leadership (Genesis 37:36; 39:1-6).

Servitude was Joseph's new normal. Yet, his sense of worth and identity remained consistent with his dreams. His lowly state of servitude was not so disheartening that it prevented him from gaining favor with Potiphar. Joseph had effectively adjusted to a new normal, while still realizing that his worth and identity were in the eyes of the Lord.

His "Falsely Accused by the Captain's Wanton Wife" Crises

Young, handsome, successful and feeling favored, Joseph's new normal was upended, due to no fault of his own. He found himself imprisoned for a crime he did not commit. Once again, he had to adjust to a different situation of life. Would being wrongly imprisoned "do Joseph in"? Being snatched from a position of power and prestige, would he adjust to a prison routine? What challenges to his sense of worth would this bring? How could "who he is to the Lord" possibly serve him in prison? Joseph's new normal would depend on the answers to these questions (Genesis 39:7-20).

His "Wrongly Imprisoned" Crises

Scripture tells us:

But while Joseph was there in the prison, the Lord was with him; he showed him kindness and granted him favor in the eyes of the prison warden. So the warden put Joseph in charge of all those held in the prison, and he was made responsible for all that was done there. The warden paid no attention to anything under Joseph's care, because the Lord was with Joseph and gave him success in whatever he did. (Genesis 39:20b-23)

Just as when Joseph had been in a well, imprisoned, the Lord was there with him. Though his situation of life had shifted, who he was to the Lord was unchanged.

Meanwhile, Pharaoh, the king of Egypt, because he was angry with his chief cupbearer and his chief baker, threw them into the same prison with Joseph. Sometime later, both chief cupbearer and his chief baker had a dream on the same night. Fortunately, Joseph was there to tell them the meaning of their dreams: the cupbearer would be reinstated, but the baker would be put to death. Later, during a feast on the Pharaoh's birthday, the chief cupbearer was set free, but the chief baker was put to death. Though the chief baker had promised to remember Joseph, he did not. There sat Joseph, forgotten in prison, without a pardon in sight.

His bunkie likely thought; *What good does it do to serve the Lord, if Joe is going to experience what everyone else experiences?* Also, Joseph may have thought; *Why me Lord? Am I a sucker for doing what's right, while others receive pleasure from doing as they please? How much longer will I spend time confined here?*

Being let down by a person whom he had helped, and perhaps devastated by the uncertainty of a new normal in confinement – due to no fault of his own – is at best a recipe for becoming perplexed (Genesis 39:20-23; 40:1-23).

His "In Charge of Pharaoh's Palace" Crises

Adjusting to the new normal of imprisonment, Joseph continued to be a blessing to the warden. Unknown to him, while seemingly left in prison for who knows how long, the Lord was orchestrating a release His way (God's ways are not our ways - Isaiah 55:8-9). The Lord had given the Egyptian Pharaoh two dreams that were so disturbing that he sent for all the magicians and wise men of Egypt to tell him their meaning, but no one could interpret them for him.

The chief cupbearer, remembering his own experience with troubling dreams, remembered Joseph and the promise he had made to him two years prior. He immediately told Pharaoh, who in turn had Joseph cleaned up and quickly brought to him from the dungeon. But when asked to interpret the Pharaoh's dream, Joseph told Pharaoh that he could not interpret the dream, but that God would provide the answer (Genesis 41:14-16).

By this, we can determine that regardless of Joseph's tears, high and low points while in prison, and any bargaining with the Lord, his trust in the Lord remained intact. Not only did he interpret Pharoah's dream, but he also provided a detailed recommendation about how Pharaoh needed to respond. Then Pharaoh said to Joseph:

> Since God has made all this known to you, there is no one so discerning and wise as you. You shall be in charge of my palace, and all my people are to submit to your orders. Only with respect to the throne will I be greater than you."
> Genesis 41:39-40

Also read Genesis 41:1-40.

Joseph did not allow cravings for familiar routines in life's normalcy to lure him away from valuing his godly worth and otherworldly identity; as obscure as those may have been to him. You see, what pleases God is our faith in His unseen promises (Hebrews 11:6). Such faith helps us stand firm as life situations shift. Over a millennium later, believers under the Lord's new covenant would be told, "being confident of this, that he who began a good work in you will carry it on to completion until the day of Christ Jesus" (Philippians 1:6).

And last …

His "Second-in-Command Over All of Egypt" Crises

Joseph's elevation did not end there. Pharaoh put him in charge of the whole land of Egypt. Then he gave Joseph his signet ring, dressed him in robes of fine linen, and put a gold chain around his neck. Joseph rode in a chariot as Pharaoh's second-in-command. As a result, during the seven years of famine, the children of Israel survived by residing near Egypt and eating grain. Joseph's father, mother, and brothers received grain from the storehouses that Joseph had built in Egypt. Prophecy fulfilled!

The following illustration depicts Joseph's life shifts and shake-ups, while he maintained integrity to, and awareness of, who he was to the Lord.

Joseph Understood His Worth and Identity Throughout His Journey

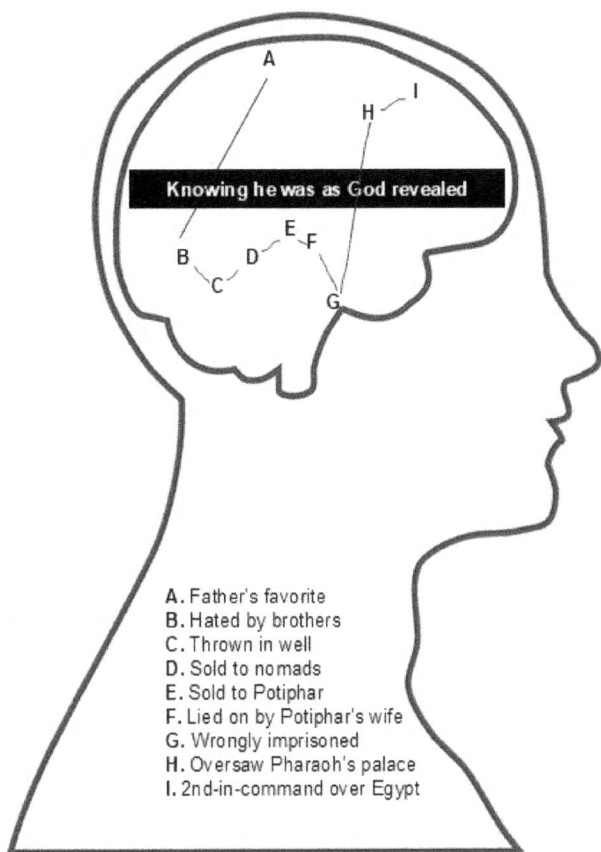

Knowing he was as God revealed

A. Father's favorite
B. Hated by brothers
C. Thrown in well
D. Sold to nomads
E. Sold to Potiphar
F. Lied on by Potiphar's wife
G. Wrongly imprisoned
H. Oversaw Pharaoh's palace
I. 2nd-in-command over Egypt

Fulfilling His Role in the Lord's Plan for Israel

Finally, the interpretation of the dreams that Joseph had told his brothers, father and mother came to fruition. In Genesis 47:11-12, after the famine, it states:

> Joseph settled his father and his brothers in Egypt and gave them property in the best part of the land, the district of Rameses, as Pharaoh directed. Joseph also provided his father and his brothers and all his father's household with food, according to the number of their children.

> Also read Genesis 41:41-49.

It is not a stretch to believe that as Joseph's sense of normalcy shifted, with each of his crises, he employed a different set of abilities and perspectives in order to adjust. Still, he did not lose sight of his worth and identity in the Lord.

Log

Chapter 1: Our Dim Understanding

For now we see only a reflection as in a mirror;
then we shall see face to face. Now I know in part;
then I shall know fully, even as I am fully known.
(1 Corinthians 13:12)

Either Joseph had unwavering belief in his godly worth and otherworldly identity, or his trust in the Lord brought peace to his uncertainty as he experienced one crisis after another. Scripture does not reveal which was the case. But from interacting with my children and grandchildren when they were younger, and now my great-grandchildren, I observed that not explaining some things to them, strengthened their dependence on me. More importantly, through dependence at their young age, they learned that I could be trusted. Perhaps the same dynamic is at work, with the Lord, during your crisis.

Because we are neither omniscient or have the cerebral capacity, there will always be a need to trust God the Father. Believers under the old covenant had to trust Him about obscure matters, as well as believers under the new covenant.

Israel's Belief in the Obscure and Otherworldly

The children of Israel at that time, believed as do traditional Jews today, that after death there will be the regathering of the Israelites from around the earth. The bodies of their dead were to rise and reunite with their souls. While alive, this promise was critical to their sense of worth and identity. They perceived the physical body to have value beyond its earthly existence (2 Kings 13:20-22, Ezekiel 37:1-14). However, there was no promise that their spirit would be quickened to life, neither while on earth nor thereafter.

Scripture reveals this belief in action during the life of Joseph, Moses and Joshua. Consider the following:

> "And Joseph made the Israelites swear an oath and said, "God will surely come to your aid, and then you must carry my bones up from this place." - Genesis 50:25

"Moses took the bones of Joseph with him because Joseph had made the Israelites swear an oath. He had said, "God will surely come to your aid, and then you must carry my bones up with you from this place." - Exodus 13:19

"And Joseph's bones, which the Israelites had brought up from Egypt, were buried at Shechem in the tract of land that Jacob bought for a hundred pieces of silver." ... - Joshua 24:32

Obscure Revelation Today and Human Omission

God the Father, in His amazing wisdom, concealed some things from human understanding during old covenant times. He later revealed more for new covenant believers to understand. But He has many more obscure things sealed, until the future, for believer's understanding. That challenges our trust.

If you think that challenges your understanding of how to live for Christ until His return, consider the following unfortunate trend on top of that. In most Western Christian church traditions, especially during the last thirty years, the subject of spirituality of the reconciled and redeemed souls has been minimized. It is so rare to hear it now, that when it is mentioned, many Christians think you mean something related to the occult, New Age or some sort of mysticism. Sermons and teachings directed to believers today sound more like self-help guidelines, positive thinking challenges, optimism, motivational talks, or a set of religious rules. And to a lesser extent, the same is true about the subject of "holiness" (being set apart).

Yet, Apostles Paul and Peter have much to say about the spiritual nature of those who are "in-Christ". (Romans 7:14-25; Romans 12:10-12; 1 Corinthians 2:10-16; 1 Corinthians 12:7-11; 1 Peter 2:4-5). When we read those scriptures, we realize that once saved there is an unexplored realm to life that relates to our worth, identity and access to divine power. We discover that the Lord views us through the lens of this spirituality, and not as others view us, nor according to our lives prior to salvation.

Holiness is not physical nor relational distancing, but it is living out this new realm of spirituality while in a sin-prone body (Romans 7:14; Romans 8:1-13), without mixing the two in our daily walk. This is the condition of being a new creation. Therefore, the use of the term *spiritual* throughout this book only refers to that realm.

This is why the author of Hebrews says that, "*without faith it is impossible to please God.*" We must trust and obey.

Christian Belief in the Obscure and Otherworldly

Through Jesus, for the first time, followers who trust Him, as Lord and Savior, would be saved (Romans 10:9-10) and imputed with the Holy Spirit (Ephesians 1:13-14). Then, through grace, they can discern truth and have the power to obey it. *Imputed* means that once you were without such power, but when you were saved, that power became internal; and extends beyond your earthly existence.

That is why your bones need not be preserved in order to reunite with your soul upon resurrection. Instead, at the moment that you believed, you became a new creature, born of the Spirit and empowered with the grace to walk in your newness for Christ. Your worth and identity are no longer rooted in past achievements or natural virtues. Instead, they ignite from your newness of life.

Here's an analogy that brings some clarity to the topic.

A Burning Log

Under the new covenant, think of our earthly body and its accomplishments as a log set aflame. Our body (the log) carries a living spirit (the flame) that has been quickened (ignited) to life by the Holy Spirit. That is called regeneration.

Our soul's responsibility is to keep the log's fire roaring, by valuing virtues that accumulate like treasures in heaven, regardless of the log's situation of life. This fire is eternal. Ignited in the log by the eternal Holy Spirit, it no longer requires the log to exist.

During our log's existence, it holds and supports the fire. When our log ceases to exist, the fire continues to flame (life eternal).

This is the correct and only focus that will enable you to benefit from our All-Knowing Lord. During times of uncertainty, He gives the provisions needed to thrive on earth, with respect for your salvific purpose. To focus more on your log will only maintain "log normalcy." Though the familiarity may bring some comfort, you will have no sense of divine presence or life purpose. It will only bind you tighter to the ebbs and flows of the nasty here and now. Neglecting the fire leads to feeling that life is meaningless. A focus on your fire is a focus on an eternal resource. It has abundant provisions.

Faith is the engine that pulls the train through life. *Understanding* is the caboose that follows.

Though Veiled in Scripture

There is so much yet to be revealed to us as kingdom believers. Scripture assures us that we will understand later (1 Corinthians 12:13). But as we journey on this earth, there may be things that will seem fuzzy.

Here is a clue that will make things clearer: The old covenant, through the preservation of a deceased body, shaped humanity's consciousness about the connection of the person's life on earth with their afterlife through resurrection. While the new covenant, through its good news about justification by faith, reveals the criteria for afterlife through resurrection – none other than Jesus Christ.

- Under both covenants, the believer's worth and identity exists beyond their earthly body, occupation, and routine.

- The souls of old covenant believers were bound by the disobedient actions of Adam. The souls of new covenant believers exist as new creations (2 Corinthians 5:17) who have been freed and empowered to choose obedience or disobedience.

Warehouse

Chapter 2: Skill Inventories

As a New Testament believer, have you tested your new capacities that come with being a new creation? Or, though saved, did you remain within those same familiar human comfort zones, designed to make you feel safe and accepted? The challenge for every believer is to embrace the unfamiliar life of our new creation, while resisting the wiles of our familiar life (which are often responsible for the crisis).

Succeeding in this challenge is crucial to thriving during times of uncertainty. Performing an inventory of your familiar life helps you to find a way through uncertainty. Consider the inventories of a manager and that of Joseph below.

The Shrewd Manager's Inventory

This manager's crisis was described in one of Jesus' parables. He worked for a rich man. But word got out that he was about to lose his job. Rather than be swallowed up by frustration, depression, anger or pity, in order to survive his pending crisis, the manager inventoried his skills.

> "The manager said to himself, 'What shall I do now? My master is taking away my job. I'm not strong enough to dig, and I'm ashamed to beg— I know what I'll do so that, when I lose my job here, people will welcome me into their houses." (Luke 16:3-4)

Joseph's Inventory

As you have read previously, throughout Joseph's shifting situations in life, he had developed diverse skills and perspectives. To name a few, he learned to tend flocks, deal with hostility, call on God to reveal the meaning of dreams, identify back-stabbing associates, trust God during life's dark and empty times, and endure betrayal by those closest to him. He understood that life can be heartless to the innocent, that having humility is essential, how to manage the affairs and business of another's household, and the value of earning trust. Joseph experienced the lies and deceit of a wanton woman. He survived incarceration, managed a prison, delivered bad news, overcame being forgotten, learned to solve problems, managed and led a nation, and finally, he learned to have mercy and to be forgiving.

Your Skill Inventory

You too have accumulated diverse skills and perspectives throughout your past. You can either view them as water under the bridge or water that fuels a hydro-powered plant. So reflect back on the times that felt certain. What did you excel in doing? What had you done that won praise from others? To what causes or conditions were you particularly sympathetic? What work tasks, skills, techniques, processes, or procedures felt enjoyable? These can be leveraged into redefining yourself for future opportunities (fueling your hydro-powered plant). Inventory your skills, and then list them. It's also a good idea to ask someone who knows.

Inventory your skills using the sample template below:

Ability #1: _____

Ability #2: _____

Ability #3: _____

Ability #4: _____

Make another list of needs that other people or employers have that align with your abilities. It's also a good idea to ask someone who knows you, and whom you trust, to suggest additional needs with which your abilities align.

Need Area A: _____

Need Area B: _____

Need Area C: _____

Alongside of your first list, using terminology common to employers or others, describe how your ability fits the need. Pray for the insight to clearly articulate how your ability can meet it. Practice saying it! Throughout your new normal of uncertainty, devote yourself to trusting the assurance that is afforded your new creation in Christ. Cease from answering the "what if" questions popping up in your mind with fear. Start embracing a curiosity about the responsibilities of a new creature in Christ. And remember, the kingdom of God has not shifted, just your temporal situation of life has. Pray for the strength to wrestle your fear under control.

Taming Uncertainty

The inherent uncertainty in any new normal will preclude you from knowing what is needed, in order to survive it. So refrain from asking for or expecting anything specific. That could add frustration upon frustration. Instead, with humility, follow what you already know about walking in step with the Lord. Anticipate being vulnerable as you reach for new goals. Prepare to be stretched beyond your comfort zones.

It is important to note that with each shift in Joseph's situation of life, a way out of it came to him. He did not manufacture it. Likewise, for you, eventually some or all that you prayed about from your inventory will be useful in the Lord's way out for you.

Here's a Lesson from the Lobster

In addition to being a defense system, a lobster's skeletal system is on the outside of its body. In order to grow, it must shed the comfort and safety of its skeleton. At that time, its soft flesh is vulnerable to treacherous creatures and elements in the sea. However, if it does not shed, its skeleton will become its tomb. In effect, lobsters have to pick a vulnerability. So, when you see that big juicy lobster in a commercial, remember, that it has taken many risks. It is the same in your situation.

Obstacles

Chapter 3: Your Worth in Divine Currency

Under the old covenant, beliefs about the general resurrection required the body of the deceased, in order for it to be raised and reunited with the person's soul. This is not the case with the bodies of deceased believers under the new covenant. While living, the bodies of new covenant believers exist to ignite and carry the fire of their living spirit (our spiritual birth). That is why we are called to be living sacrifices. Our soul and spirit transcend death. They will be given a new and glorified body upon Jesus' return.

Regardless of socioeconomic status, wealth, health or political affiliation, while on Earth, our experiences make more sense when we view ourselves as migrant living sacrifices, being renewed daily by the Holy Spirit. Our worth is measured in divine currency, which often has very little value in this life. Yet, Jesus suggests that, while on earth, we remain mindful of our heavenly treasure account (Matthew 6:19-20) until His return.

How are we migrants?

The bible calls for every believer in Jesus Christ to make an introspective migration. It is not in terms of time or space, but from a self-centered soul that has been shaped by sin, to a Christ-centered perspective with an eternal outlook.

Gaining Assurance

The migration aligns with the new worth and identity that came with your salvation. Religious confusion will exist if you expect assurances from new worth and identity, while still centered on the comforts and sins of self. God is not the source of confusion. Until you were saved, your life was being shaped by sin. So there are many obstacles within that are preventing you from migrating. None of them are too difficult for the Holy Spirit to help you navigate. The degree to which you keep in step with the Holy Spirit directly determines the degree to which those obstacles are overcome. And you will experience assurance about your worth and identity to the extent that you are overcoming those obstacles.

The journey to a Christ-centered perspective begins with salvation. Thereafter, should you choose to migrate (yes, you can choose not to, and still remain loved and forgiven by the Lord), your obedience to God's Word and trust the power of His Spirit will be essential for overcoming obstacles.

Faith pleases the Lord (Hebrews 11:6). The greater your faith, the greater your discernment. With greater discernment you will better understand and accept the ways of the Lord. It is similar to when a teenager demonstrates responsible driving and decision-making. It is then; that they can handle having their own car. Or, when they demonstrate that they can make good financial decisions, they can properly handle receiving larger sums of money. Likewise, as you grow in faith along this journey, you will see the Lord more clearly. The more clearly you see Him, the more appreciation you will have for your new worth and identity in Christ and develop a kingdom perspective.

Becoming obedient to God's Word is in your hands. This booklet cannot help with that. Nor can it help you develop trust in the power of the Holy Spirit. Those are your sacrificial offerings to the Lord. What this booklet does is provide guidance around or through the obstacles that could prevent you from completing the migratory journey.

Let's Consider Four Obstacles to Overcome

- Obstacle #1: Assurance Rooted in Doing, Rather than Being

  Your doing can be an obstacle to your *being*. Confusion around who you are in Christ and what you are called do on the job, in the community, with family, in relationships, and in intimate situations can lead to doubts about your sense of worth or identity in Christ. The truth is, there is nothing you can do to earn kingdom worth. Likewise, there is no protocol to follow that would establish your identity in Christ.

The simple act of turning your life over to Christ causes you to *be* a new creature. On this journey, there is nothing you can do to be separated from God's love (Romans 8:38-39). You were called to *be* a disciple, not merely *do* discipling. By grace, through faith, you have become a joint heir with Christ.

Every believer has been called to discipleship. Those who submit to the call do so from a place of gratitude, not obligation or fear. That gratitude is grounded in love towards Jesus for redeeming them. That is the proper response to our Lord. We show hatred for heavenly authority (in our decision-making, not necessarily in our hearts) when we do not show love in this manner. Heaven has no tolerance for an *I like to do things my way* mindset. Discipleship is essential to every believer, not just your church leaders.

- Obstacle #2: Worldly Understanding of Success
  The prosperity gospel and some general "church talk" often wrongly ties worldly success, or the lack of it, to a person's relationship with God. At least, that is how it is often interpreted. When a believer falls into economic despair or suffers a significant loss, the assumption is often that he or she is not living right. That is missing-link logic. The fallacy in such reasoning is this: Any worldly success that believers experience is due to

God's grace (unmerited favor), and is to be leveraged to benefit God's kingdom. No one has earned anything good from God. It is only because He is good that we are granted any good thing.

Similarly, when an impoverished believer seeks ways to benefit God's kingdom, in spite of their circumstances, they can expect the Lord's provisions. Not because they earned it, but because the Lord promised to do so out of His compassion. You need only to watch a national news channel to know that it is foolish to grade a believer's relationship with God based on the fragility of earthly success. Your relationship with God is kingdom based, where economic uncertainty, wars, crises, politics, or death have no effect.

- Obstacle #3: Treating This Life as Home
  Your life on Earth, as taught by God's Word, is that of a sojourner or stranger (Hebrews 11:13-16). Attempts to make it home will certainly lead to disappointment. Because, not only has the Earth been corrupted by Adam's sin, but also because what you and others desire from this life has been corrupted by the same. Even as you do good, sin is present! (Romans 7:21-25) That is why the Bible urges you to embrace discipleship to experience a change in perspective (Romans 12:1-2).

But wouldn't living like a stranger make us vulnerable in so many ways, thereby creating more uncertainty?

It would, if our sense of worth or our understanding of who we are is rooted in this world. Even Jesus knew we would be vulnerable. That is why He made it a key point, while praying to the Father just before the arrest that led to His crucifixion (John 17:14). God the Father will honor Jesus' request. Therefore, although you are vulnerable, you are also protected while migrating as a stranger in this life. This is also why the bible can urge believers to live by faith, not by sight (2 Corinthians 5:7).

We are in this world as ordinary, yet forgiven, people who do all sorts of things such as - studies, deliveries, software engineering, policing, teaching, clerking, etc. Yet, our worth and identity are not of this world. Rather, they are of God's kingdom. The more you embrace life on Earth like a stranger, who occupies Earth until Jesus returns, the more in tune you will be with your true worth and the more clearly you will understand who you were created to be (your identity). This makes for a peaceful journey!

- Obstacle #4: Fear and Doubt

Fear of the consequences of embracing Christ-centered principles, and doubting the Lord's promises are the roars of a toothless and clawless lion. The evil one has unleashed them to prevent you from believing in your kingdom worth and knowing your kingdom identity. He hopes you will perceive the journey to be meaningless or silly and never embrace the blessings inherent in the belief that Jesus urged in John 20:29, where He says:

> " … Because you have seen me, you have believed; blessed are those who have not seen and yet have believed."

In Matthew 4:1-11, Jesus was tempted while in the wilderness. There, He demonstrated how to deal with the roars of fear and doubt from the evil one. To each of the devil's temptations, Jesus used Scripture to refute them. Jesus, who is the Living Word, relied upon the written word to make the devil flee from Him. So, how much more should you rely on both to refute fear and doubt when they arise.

The objective of the evil one is for fear and doubt to render your faith lukewarm towards the promises and teachings in God's Word. He does not want you on this journey!

- Predisposed to Complacency and Compromise

When times were predictable, it was so easy to minimize the value of our spiritual walk with the Lord. Without thinking about it, we took comfort, provisions, health, relationships and security for granted. For me, it was so easy to descend down that slippery slope! Then the resulting complacency quickly led to compromise.

If that is your experience as well, then you probably remember realizing just how far you fell from vows or religious convictions, that you had made with a sincere heart. This particular obstacle can easily go undetected. So while on the journey, you will need to be intentional about doing a self-examination. And then, be honest with yourself, confess and repent.

Tip in the Book of Revelation

It is not just you that the evil one is trying to prevent you from completing the journey. His worldwide plan is to make sure you do not have a testimony that would help others. A believer's testimony to another believer who is struggling, can be a powerful weapon for overcoming the evil one.

The evil one believes he can steal victory from our returning King (Jesus). But Revelation 12:10b-11 states this about the power of your testimony:

For the accuser of our brothers and sisters,

who accuses them before our God, day and
night, has been hurled down.
They triumphed over him
by the blood of the Lamb
and by the word of their testimony;
they did not love their lives so much
as to shrink from death.

Aside from praising the Lord, the two best things you
can do in this life to overcome the evil one are, 1)
trust the power of Jesus' bloodshed sacrifice, and 2)
give your testimony about what the power of the
cross redeemed you from.

Fork

Chapter 4: How and When to Migrate?

How can you migrate from a self-focused point of view, where your worth and identity have been based on what you have *done* (career, academics, personal achievements, financial status, etc.), to where your worth and identity are grounded in *being* - in Christ?

First be Willing to Submit

The truth is, some "fork-in-the-road" life situation usually compels a person to make this decision. It could be the loss of social status, death of a provider, end of a career (voluntarily or involuntarily), reduction of income, conviction of conscience, war, natural disaster, etc. Then, after enduring one failed attempt after another trying to maintain a sense of normalcy, we appeal to the Lord as a last resort.

That is when we discover that it is not about our doing (will power), but about something we rarely slow down to consider: submitting to God's Spirit and trusting His Word. A *willingness* to submit, not the ability, is how the migration begins.

As much as I want to assure you that things will go well thereafter, I cannot because they probably will not, at least initially. Another truth is, that it is essential that self-pride dies, which is often a grueling, repulsive and emotionally painful experience. This is not so much because being humble is difficult, but because of how much significance we have placed in our pride. The more pride we have, the more painful its demise. Given the lives of prominent individuals in the Bible, as well as my own personal experiences, with the Lord's help, I know that migrating is certainly doable, but at a cost. And the ways of the Lord can be quite strange at times.

Then Commence to Migrate!

Begin your migration by prayerfully asking the Lord for help with pride. Be honest about your attachment to it. Acknowledge that you have taken the credit for things, but now you realize that your success was due to His grace. Admit to being powerless against giving up prideful thoughts, and express your need for Him to decrease your appetite for self-pride, and to increase your appetite for humility and for giving Him glory for all things. Pray this regularly!

You are well into your migratory journey when being a Christian grows from mere philosophical agreement with the Bible, to denying your old self its sinful desires, as you obey Jesus' teachings (Luke 9:23). At some point, you will choose to use your natural abilities, politics, citizenship, personal ambitions, and accomplishments to serve your new worth and identity as a citizen of God's kingdom. When this happens, you are not admitting defeat, but rather you are viewing life through a kingdom lens. Keep journeying!

Paralysis

Chapter 5: Failure to Migrate

Not every confessed Christian will step out to migrate. Some smother the Spirit's "fire" whenever it ignites something in them. Others become overwhelmed by the cares of life. There are those, deceived by the chase for wealth, who leave little or no time, energy or resources for stoking the Spirit's fire. My hope is that, what I say about three particular types of uncertainty will bring enough clarity, that taking the risk to migrate will appear worthwhile.

Uncertainty About Jesus' Trustworthiness

You will not thrive effectively during uncertain times, if you are uncertain about your standing with the Savior (who is most trustworthy). This is true whether you are uncertain about your need for Jesus, or uncertain about His acceptance of you. Either way, the notion of migrating from self-centeredness to Christ-centeredness will not even be part of your equation for surviving a crisis.

Let us dive into two other types of uncertainty. They are the two sides on the of coin of "passive rebellion." Sounds harsh, huh? Though both seem genuinely innocent, their effect almost always results in some incongruity with the Lord. Every person redeemed by the blood of Jesus was saved to make this migration, but for God's purpose (Ephesians 2:8-10). Before being saved, we were headed for the certainty of hell. We did nothing to deserve salvation. As stated earlier, it is out of gratitude, that we should desire to live for the Lord's purposes.

Uncertainty About Your Need for Jesus

Everyone has sinned and will certainly do so again. I believe that by societal standards, most people attending church are relatively good. Throughout their lives, they have not amassed long police rap sheets, they follow social norms, are polite most of the time, support their church and are neighborly. This is not to suggest all other people are bad. I just want to interject that, when it comes to salvation, societal good is not good enough.

Lulled into a false sense of security, many "good" people are out of touch with just how disgusting their sin is to the Lord. Unfortunately, their false sense of security leads to the false belief that they really have not done anything so bad that Jesus needed to lose His life for their forgiveness. This is rebellion through presumed compliance. It inhibits migration when the person becomes depressed due to their inability to reconcile being in a crisis, given how good they believe they have been for so long.

Uncertainty About Jesus' Acceptance

This believer is more honest about their sinful condition than the previous believer. They are very much in touch with the consensual dirt they have slung! However, their fear is; *If even my name is in the same conversation with God's, not to mention if I am standing in the same room, He's gonna strike me down hard with shame and punishment! So I'm good staying right here … self-centered ... I ain't trying to get cursed.* This is rebellion through defiance. From their perspective, not migrating is due to them not wanting to "catch a case with God".

There are so many people like this, even some who are attending church. Whether it is an unwillingness to be where the gospel is presented, or the gospel is not being presented where they attend, this person is like a grape dying on the vine. Their heart is where it needs to be, but life-giving sap is not reaching it. They will not thrive during times of uncertainty.

Fire

Chapter 6: Be the Log, Serve Your Fire!

How ever and whenever you begin to look at yourself and your situation of life through the lens of Christ, that is how and when you migrate. It is then that your earthly existence becomes as a log upon which the spirit (as fire) ignites. Your fire (with your new worth and identity) is eternal. It ceases to need the log to sustain it. Since you have been united with Christ, your fire will burn in this life and continue into the next.

Your earthly life is the log that serves your fire until the log gets consumed. The fire continues by drawing from the lifegiving sustenance of the Lord. He has always intended that your stake be in Him. Nothing is wrong with careers, wealth, life pursuits, achievements, etc. in this life. But just as Joseph did, always remember who the Lord says you are. In this life, remember to be a log who exists to serve and support the fire containing your true worth and identity in the Lord's kingdom.

Keep your fire roaring by prayerfully using your skill inventory to redefine yourself for new situations. Trust the Lord to open doors that utilize your ability. Then serve there, like you are working for the Lord Himself.

Diamond

Closing: Don't Waste Your Life Crisis

We have all been raised to find identity and purpose in temporal things. Doing so in a crisis is disastrous. Note: Your dignity has not been taken away. In fact, you have been a new creation since the day you first accepted Jesus as your Lord and Savior. Perhaps you just have not valued its worth, and therefore you missed out on owning your true worth. You may not see it right now, but the crisis is an opportunity to embrace who you actually are in the sight of the Lord, perhaps for the very first time. So do not waste this crisis. Explore what your identity in Christ has for you, by migrating to Christ-centered living. Do not just passively go to church. Jump into the fray of its kingdom life.

The experiences, accomplishments, education and relationships in your past have not been a waste. They are a great source of lessons learned, testimonies and advice to give, leverage, and insight as you migrate and redefine yourself.

Consider this: If someone discussed the principles of pressure, time, and coal as a mineral, it may bore you. But if they discussed how those can work together to bring forth new worth and new identity as a diamond, it just might hold your attention.

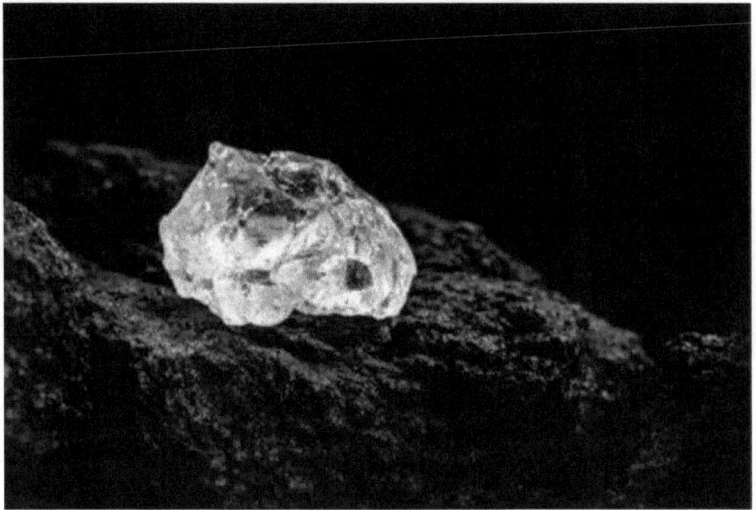

Likewise, as long as you continue to judge yourself by the temporal standards of this world, during uncertain times, you will feel a loss of dignity, used, worthless, and confused about who you are and your life's purpose. When, in fact, the Lord sees you as a work-in-progress. Like a lump of coal, under pressure, over time becomes a diamond. So heed following warning and encouragement from Jesus.

"I have told you these things, so that in me you may have peace. In this world you will have trouble. But take heart! I have overcome the world." John 16:33

About the Author

Pastor Jimmie D. Compton, Jr and his wife Nancy have two children, two grandchildren, and two great-grandchildren. Received his Masters of Arts degree in Pastoral Counseling at Ashland Theological Seminary, and was licensed as a therapist. He founded and served as Senior Pastor of Hope Bible Fellowship Church for thirty years. Pastor Compton also provided counseling services while with the Detroit Police Chaplain Corps, Detroit Rescue Mission Ministries and Eastwood Clinic. He has aided other church leaders with counseling and ministerial needs, while authoring several books.

Pastor Compton has been honored for completing in-depth, six-year research into Early African Church History: From Jesus' Birth to the Rise of Islam. This research has been embraced by church leaders and developed into a two-year, online, self-paced curriculum by Hope Institute, the teaching and ministerial arm of Hope Bible Fellowship Church.

For more information, or for bulk copies of this book at a discount, email us with "About TDUT" in the subject at hbf.church@gmail.com.

Notable Mentions About the Author

inkBlaze Media's review of Pastor Compton's book, _In All Things, Love: Escaping the Church Schism Cycle_ - "addresses pressing issues within the modern Christian Church, reflecting on historical parallels while offering a transformative perspective rooted in Jesus' kingdom message. Your book's deep exploration of these topics resonates profoundly in today's cultural and religious climate.

Your ability to blend historical analysis with actionable wisdom and personal narrative creates a compelling and relatable reading experience. The board was especially impressed by how you shed light on complex theological and cultural dynamics with clarity and passion.

With a background as a pastor, counselor, and community leader, your insights are not only well-informed but also grounded in decades of practical ministry and leadership. Your unique journey—from Detroit's eastside to a respected voice of faith—brings authenticity and authority to your work.

www.ingramcontent.com/pod-product-compliance
Lightning Source LLC
Chambersburg PA
CBHW060537030426
42337CB00021B/4310